Stevie

A Play

by Hugh Whitemore

From the life and work of
Stevie Smith

FOR AMATEUR PRODUCTION ENQUIRIES

UNITED KINGDOM AND WORLD EXCLUDING NORTH AMERICA
plays@SamuelFrench-London.co.uk
020 7255 4302/01

Each title is subject to availability from Samuel French,

depending upon country of performance.

Stevie was first presented by Duncan C. Weldon and Louis I. Michaels in association with Bullfinch Productions at the Vaudeville Theatre, London, in March 1977, with the following cast of characters:

STEVIE   Glenda Jackson
AUNT   Mona Washbourne
MAN   Peter Eyre

Director   Clifford Williams
Setting   John Gunter

Revived at Hampstead Theatre Main Stage on 6th March 2015 with the following cast:

STEVIE   Zoë Wanamaker
AUNT   Lynda Baron
MAN   Chris Larkin

Director   Christopher Morahan
Designer   Simon Higlett
Lighting   Tim Mitchell
Sound   John Leonard

The action takes place in the sitting room of Stevie's home at 1 Avondale Road, Palmers Green

ACT I: 1950 approximately
ACT II: I960 approximately

ACT I

The cluttered sitting room of a small semi-detached house in North London. Late afternoon.

There is a square bay-window with lace curtains, an upright piano covered with piles of books, a bureau and a mirror. Vases of dried rushes and honesty stand on tables alongside pot plants and flowers. Antimacassars are draped over the well-worn chairs. There are a number of amateur watercolours and some framed sepia photographs hanging on the walls.

*Upstage, **STEVIE**'s **AUNT** is watering the pot plants. She is a formidable old lady, with iron-grey hair standing upright in a fan-shaped frill. She is wearing a dress brightly patterned with flowers. The **MAN** stands by the chair offstage down right. He wears neutral, sombre clothes.*

MAN Life is like a railway station, Stevie said. The train of birth brings us in, the train of death will carry us away. All aboard for a day in the country. *(He sits in the chair)*

*The **AUNT** continues to water the pot plants.*

STEVIE *(off)* I'm back! *(She slams the front door)* I'm back! Where are you ?

AUNT In here.

***STEVIE** enters, carrying a handbag and a plastic shopping bag. She is a small, hunched, bird-like woman, with a fringe of dark, straight hair. Her pale face has an expressive mobility, and her gestures are quick, with the spontaneity of a child. She is wearing a wine-coloured corduroy pinafore dress, with heavy-knit stockings and sandals. She kisses **AUNT**.*

You're home nice and early.

STEVIE I'm utterly exhausted, worn to a frazzle. *(She puts her carrier-bag and handbag on the chaise and starts to take her coat off)*

AUNT The kettle's on, I'll make a pot of tea.

STEVIE Is there anything to eat?

AUNT Battenburg cake and some ginger nuts.

STEVIE How lovely!

AUNT Give me your coat.

STEVIE Has anything happened today?

AUNT Nothing out of the ordinary.

> **AUNT** *takes* **STEVIE**'s *coat, and exits.*

STEVIE When I'm asked at the Day of Judgement what I remember best and what has ruled my whole life, I think I shall say: "Being tired, too tired for words."

> **STEVIE** *sits at the desk chair and opens letters.*

I've been at the BBC, recording a story. I don't know why I bothered, it was a complete waste of time. The producer seemed to have quite a different idea about the story from mine. We got more and more at cross purposes, and a Mr Hall, who was sitting on the floor listening, said he couldn't make head or tail of it.

> **AUNT** *enters, carrying a plate of cake and ginger nuts.*

AUNT Head or tail of what? *(She puts the plate on the coffee table)*

STEVIE This is my aunt.

AUNT Who are you talking about?

STEVIE His name was Mr Hall.

AUNT Head or tail of *what?*

STEVIE A short story I'd written.

AUNT Poor man, I know how he felt. *(She looks for her glasses)*

STEVIE I call her the "Lion of Hull". She looks very lion-like, don't you think?

AUNT is still searching amongst the books on the piano.

The dress is new, by the way. It reminds me of one of those seed packets, you know, Carter's Tested Seeds. I call it "Every One Came Up".

AUNT Where are my glasses, Peggy?

STEVIE In the fruit bowl.

AUNT All these books, just look at them!

STEVIE Not a literary person, thank God.

AUNT *(finding her glasses)* I've never seen so much stuff and nonsense in all my life.

AUNT exits.

STEVIE *(sitting on the chaise)* Stuff and nonsense are the twin bogies of my dear Aunt's existence, and she tilts against these pet windmills with all the courage of a latter-day Don Quixote. "Stuff and Nonsense" is her call to arms, her battle cry.

AUNT enters, carrying the tea tray.

AUNT *(putting the tray on the pouffe)* That stupid kitchen tap needs a new washer. Tarnation take it.

AUNT goes to her chair.

Where's my cushion?

STEVIE Here, sorry.

STEVIE *takes the cushion from the chaise and gives it to* AUNT.

AUNT You can never find anything in this house.

AUNT *pours the tea.*

STEVIE Smart writing people think it's not at all chic to live in the suburbs with an aunt, but I don't care what they think. I've never cared about chic things, fashion and so on. What does it matter? I love Aunt and Aunt loves me. That's what really matters.

AUNT Tea, dear?

STEVIE Thank you, darling.

STEVIE *takes a tea cup from* AUNT, *who settles into her chair.* STEVIE *sits on the chaise and sips tea.*

AUNT Good?

STEVIE Mmm! Well now, where shall I begin?

AUNT Begin at the beginning and go through to the end, that's what I always say.

STEVIE Yes, and quite right too. Well. The twentieth of September, nineteen hundred and two: that was the beginning for me. The twentieth of September. Virgo. Rather a prim sign I always think, so I like to pretend I'm a bit of a Libra, too.

AUNT A Yorkshire lass, born in Hull. Thirty-four, Delapole Avenue, such a nice house.

STEVIE We left when I was only three, so I don't remember much about it. Just wearing a pale blue coat, and having strawberries and cream on a vast stretch of bright green grass with people in white on it.

AUNT A Cricket Club tea.

STEVIE It must've been, yes. And so, on an autumn afternoon in nineteen hundred and six, my mother, my aunt, my five-year-old sister Molly and I arrived here in Palmers Green.

AUNT All those years ago! It doesn't seem possible.

STEVIE She was a romantic girl, my mama, and because of this she made what they call an "unsuitable" marriage.

AUNT If your grandma had lived your mother and father would never have met, let alone married.

STEVIE And where would Stevie have been then, poor thing?

AUNT He was a great believer in independence, your grandfather. "Decide for yourself," he was always saying, and that's just what she did.

The front door knocker bangs.

There's my paper.

AUNT *exits.*

STEVIE My Mother was a romantic girl
So she had to marry a man with his hair in curl
Who subsequently became my unrespected papa,
But that was a long time ago now.

AUNT *enters with the newspaper and sits reading.*

What folly it is that daughters are always supposed to be
In love with papa. It wasn't the case with me.
I couldn't take to him at all
But he took to me
What a sad fate to befall
A child of three.

I sat upright in my baby carriage
And wished mama hadn't made such a foolish marriage.

I tried to hide it, but it showed in my eyes unfortunately
And a fortnight later papa ran away to sea.

He used to come home on leave
It was always the same
I could not grieve
But I think I am somewhat to blame.

AUNT Kent are doing badly: eighty-five for six.

STEVIE So with my father sailing the seven seas, we came here to Avondale Road. When we had settled ourselves in, we went round the corner to our landlord's shop, he was a plumber, a tall, thin man who looked like Charles the Second, we went round the corner to make some arrangements and to get me weighed.

AUNT You were always being weighed for one reason or another.

STEVIE He had some enormous weighing machines, I remember, the sort they use for luggage.

AUNT "You're a fine package", he said, lifting you onto the scales. "I came on a train," you said, "on a train, and then on a tram." And so you did, bless your heart.

STEVIE He was wrong, that plumber. I wasn't a fine package at all. I was always being ill.

AUNT That's why I came to London. Someone had to look after you, with your mother being so weak and poorly.

STEVIE Yes, I often wish I'd been a bright, healthy child, but I wasn't and that's that. Fate, I suppose. Stevie's fate.

AUNT Fate, indeed!

STEVIE I believe in fate, I really do.

MAN It's like a man playing cards, Stevie said. There's the man himself, and the cards he's playing, and there's another man watching over his shoulder. The player is life, the watcher is the spirit, and the cards are fate. Stevie's fate was unfortunate, to say the least. It was tuberculosis.

STEVIE *lights a cigarette.*

STEVIE I spent months and months in a children's hospital, and actually thought of suicide for the first time when I was eight. The thought cheered me up wonderfully. "Life may be treacherous," I remember thinking to myself, "But you can always rely upon Death." It also occurred to me that if one can remove oneself from the world at any time, why particularly *now*? I realized that Death is my servant; he has got to come if I call him. I think every sensitive young child should learn this. It's a great source of strength and comfort.

AUNT Love nest vicar jailed for three years. Fancy that. Serve him right.

They laugh.

STEVIE Eventually I got better, and came back home to Avondale Road.
How sweet the birds of Avondale,
Of Avondale, of Avondale,
How sweet the birds of Avondale
Do swoop and sing and call.

My sister and I thought it a very beautiful house and a beautiful garden, and so it was, so it is. Although our cautious elders would at first only sign a lease for six months, we've lived here ever since. *(Rising)* Mind you, it was a country place then, with woods going all the way up to Southgate Station, but I still find it very dreamy and poetical. The people are charming too. They have a non-interfering helpful politeness, which is rather like old Chinese courtesy.

AUNT Is it six o'clock yet?

STEVIE Twenty to.

AUNT Soon be time to do the vegetables.

> **STEVIE** *glances at the vase of bulrushes that stands on the piano.*

STEVIE I picked those bulrushes when I was a girl. Molly and I found them in the dark, mysterious, wonderful woods where Trespassers were Forbidden. They've been here almost as long as I have. *(She smiles as memories flood into her mind)* How well I remember it, how clearly! A ripe September time with the autumn sunshine in the air and the rich smell of acorns and damp mould and the Michaelmas daisies, especially there was the smell of the large Michaelmas daisies that grew in the churchyard. Of course it wasn't always September or always sunny, but that's how one is apt to remember past times, don't you think?

MAN There never were so many poppies as there were then, So much yellow corn, so many fine days, Such sharp bright air, such seas.

STEVIE This sunny time of a happy childhood seems now like a golden age; a time untouched by war, a dream of innocent quiet happenings, a dream in which people go quietly about their blameless business, bringing their garden marrows to the Harvest Festival, believing in peace, believing in progress—providing it was progress in the right direction— and believing in God. Believing also that the horrible things of life always happen abroad or to the undeserving poor, and that no good comes from brooding upon them. Oh yes, I was happy then. Very happy.

> Mother, I love you so,
> Said the child, I love you more than I know.
> She laid her head on her mother's arm
> And the love between them kept them warm.

> **AUNT** *emerges from behind her newspaper.*

AUNT More tea, Peggy?

STEVIE Yes, please.

> **AUNT** *refills the tea cups.*

> Two old ladies lived next door to us in those days.

AUNT Miss Jessie and Miss Emily.

STEVIE Miss Jessie used to do a lot of work for missionary organizations and was always collecting clothes "for the 'eathen". She was a happy, cheerful person, unlike her sister, who was full of doom and disaster. It was from her, from Miss Emily, that we first learnt about the White Slave Traffic.

AUNT Yes, your mother was very cross about it. "I've told you, Peggy," I remember your mother saying to you, "I've told you never to speak to strangers in the street or to take sweets from them. So run along and do as I tell you and don't worry your head about the White Slave Traffic."

STEVIE But it was too late. Miss Emily had fired my imagination. "If a lady comes up to you," she said, "if a lady comes up to you in a closed cab and leans out of the window and asks you to get in, don't you have anything to do with her." Then she seized my hand, and pulled me close up to her. I can remember her old lady smell now: the lavender and the moth-balls, the dusty velvet ribbon and the menthol lozenges she used to suck and, sometimes, the faint smell of her old dog clinging about her skirt. "Don't you have anything to do with her," she'd say, "it's the White Slave Traffic." But what would happen if you yielded to the blandishments of this strange lady in a closed cab? Ah, that we did not know. I remember for a long time I used to think that the wax work child models displaying clothes in the draper's shop windows were really the white slave children who had been changed into statues, and that here indeed might truly be discerned the sinister hand of the white slavers.

AUNT I've never heard such nonsense.

STEVIE May be not, but I believed every word of it.

AUNT Stuff and nonsense. You should've known better.

STEVIE I wasn't very old, was I? Seven or eight, at the most.

AUNT Old enough to know better. You were at school, after all.

STEVIE That's right, so I was. So I was. Schoolgirl Stevie. *(She laughs: a long, raucous chuckle)* We had the most unusual headmistress, I remember. *(She turns to her* **AUNT***)*

What was her name?

AUNT What was whose name?

STEVIE Our headmistress; tall woman, with glasses.

AUNT I've no idea, quite forgotten.

STEVIE Well it doesn't matter. She was a Quaker lady, I remember that; a Quaker lady with a real devotion for teaching. She believed in discipline, and she had a high, some people might think a rather simple, moral code, and she used to recite her own moralistic verses at morning prayers:

I wish that I were some beautiful land
Called the Land of Beginning Again,
Where all our mistakes and all our heartaches,
All of our poor foolish pain,
Could be dropped like a shabby coat at the door
And never put on again.
No, never more.

AUNT Oh, that's rather good.

STEVIE We didn't like that one very much. We thought it was rather sloppy. But there was a fine touch of melodrama about one of our headmistress's chief favourites, which went something like this:

Tomorrow, she told her conscience,
Tomorrow I mean to be good,
Tomorrow I'll do as I ought,
Tomorrow I'll think as I should,
Tomorrow I'll conquer the passions
That keep me from heaven away;
But ever her conscience whispered
One word and one only: Today!

Tomorrow, tomorrow, tomorrow,
And thus through the years it went on;
Tomorrow, tomorrow, tomorrow,
Till youth like a shadow was gone,
Till age and her passions had written
The message of fate on her brow,
And forth from the shadows came Death
With the terrible syllable: NOW!

STEVIE *laughs, rocking back and forth, with her hands covering her face.*

Oh yes, we liked that one. Our headmistress, like other more professional readers of verse, didn't pull her punches when it was a matter of expression. That NOW! fairly shocked us all.

AUNT *lowers her newspaper.*

AUNT There's a piece here about a man who owes the Income Tax people twenty-five thousand pounds. Twenty-five thousand! They were on to me fast enough last year. Twelve pounds short, and they were on to me fast enough. The devils!

AUNT *returns to her newspaper.*

STEVIE Like most of the class, I was devoted to our form
mistress, a wonderful lady who combined geography
with painting, and subsequently left us for ever to study
Egyptology under Flinders Petrie. "Now, children,"
she'd say, "Have you got any large hat boxes or dress
boxes at home?" Yes, yes our mamas had plenty of such
boxes. "Then bring them along with you tomorrow,
and bring some moss to lay in the bottom of the box
and then we can begin our jungle scene." The next
day we'd set to work in earnest, painting the insides
of our box lids rich indigos and blues, ochres and
greens until they looked to our inspired imaginations
exactly like the jungles of a tropical forest, I've loved
the tropics ever since—although I had and still have a
horror of snakes.

AUNT Oh, I don't like snakes.

MAN Dearest Evelyn, I often think of you
Out with the guns in the jungle stew
Yesterday I hittapotamus
I put the measurements down for you but they got lost
in the fuss
It's not a good thing to drink out here
You know, I've practically given it up dear.
Tomorrow I am going alone a long way
Into the jungle. It is all grey
But green on top
Only sometimes when a tree has fallen
The sun comes down plop, it is quite appalling.
You never want to go in a jungle pool
In the hot sun, it would be the act of a fool
Because it's always full of anacondas, Evelyn, not
looking ill-fed
I'll say. So no more now, from your loving husband,
Wilfred.

AUNT *folds her newspaper and stands up. She picks up the tea tray.*

AUNT Beans or carrots, Peggy?

STEVIE What are we having? *(She puts her cup on the tray)*

AUNT Lamb.

STEVIE Beans, then, please.

AUNT Open the door will you, love. Beans it is.

STEVIE *opens the door.*

AUNT *exits with the tray.*

STEVIE Actually, I was rather *mal vue* at school, and I'm sure with reason, though I'd rather have been thought naughty than stupid. I think perhaps I was too easily bored. Sometimes, even now, I indulge in the utmost limit of boredom, so that when the telephone rings it's like an Angel of Grace breaking in on the orgy of boredom to which my soul is committed. But by and large I'm a forward looking girl and don't stay where I am. "Left, right, be bright", as I said in a poem. That's on the days when I'm one big bounce, and have to go careful so as not to be a nuisance. Above all, I try to avoid getting too despairing. I try to remember what they said in the thirteen hundreds: "Accidie poisons the soul stream."

MAN Rapunzel Rapunzel let down your hair
It is I your beautiful lover who am here
And when I come up this time I will bring a rope ladder with me
And then we can both escape into the dark wood immediately.

STEVIE Cool as a cucumber calm as a mill pond sound as a bell
Was Mary when she went to the Wishing Well.

She has not been seen since then
If you ask me she'll not be seen again.

MAN I am a frog
I live under a spell
I live at the bottom
Of a green well.

I have been a frog now
For a hundred years
And in all this time
I have not shed many tears.

I am happy, I like the life,
Can swim for many a mile
—When I have hopped to the river—
And am for ever agile.

STEVIE 'Twas the voice of the Wanderer, I heard
her exclaim,
You have weaned me too soon, you must nurse
me again,
She taps as she passes at each window pane,
Pray, does she not know that she taps in vain?

MAN No man has seen her, this pitiful ghost,
And no woman either, but heard her at most,
Sighing and tapping and sighing again,
You have weaned me too soon, you must nurse me
again.

STEVIE Yes, there's a lot of sadness in these childhood
poems, I'm afraid, but that's because one soon realizes
how brief it all is: schooldays, summer holidays by the
seaside, those cloudless September afternoons. Sooner
or later adult fears are bound to seep in. Heigh-ho,
indeed they are. Sooner or later you're bound to
realize that you're just another human being, nothing
special, just an ordinary mortal like everyone else.
What a terrifying moment that is.

MAN You are only one of many
And of small account if any
You think about yourself too much.
This touched the child with a quick touch
And worked his mind to such a pitch
He threw his fellows in a ditch
This little child
That was so mild
Is grown too wild.

Murder in the first degree, cries Old Fury
Recording the verdict of the jury.
Now they are come to the execution tree.
The gallows stand wide. Ah me, ah me.

Christ died for sinners, intoned the Prison
Chaplain from his miscellany.
Weeping bitterly the little child cries:
I die one of many.

STEVIE I was still very young when my mother died. She had suffered greatly. Poor dear mama, she made an unsuitable marriage, and no doubt my father found it unsuitable too. Unsuitable marriages breed the Stevies of this world, and a lot of other troubles as well.

AUNT *enters, carrying a bowl of beans and a knife.*

AUNT The rat died, did I tell you? *(She puts the beans on the pouffe)*

STEVIE What rat?

AUNT The one who lived in the garden. *(She sits)* He used to sit by the fence, grinding his teeth. Big as a dog he was, I got quite fond of him, poor old fellow. The dustmen heaved a brick at him. "That's done for him," they said. And so it had. Poor old fellow.

AUNT *begins to slice the beans.*

Where have you got to?

STEVIE Nineteen-eighteen.

AUNT The end of the war.

STEVIE Mother's heart attack.

AUNT Ah, yes.

STEVIE She'd had heart trouble for many years, and wasn't
the happiest of people, alas.
I have a happy nature,
But mother is always sad,
I enjoy every moment of my life,
Mother has been had.

Well, that's not entirely true. I often feel sea sad myself,
loamishly sad, like Tennyson, with a sadness too deep
for words.

AUNT Just like your poor mother, though she had every
reason to be sad. Your grandpa was a very impatient
man, and he had no patience with your mother, not a
scrap; he thought she was a peevish, dreamy child. Not
that he was cruel, you mustn't think that, he was just
thoughtless. He'd be unkind without meaning to be
unkind. He'd laugh at your mother's fancies because
he didn't understand them. I remember him laughing
at the paintings she brought home from school.

STEVIE I can't understand people who don't care for
paintings, I can't understand them at all. *(She takes a
book on Tintoretto from the bookcase and squats beside* AUNT,
showing her the picture) My top favourite is in Venice,
it's by Tintoretto, and it's called 'The Creation of the
World'. It's a marvellous painting! There are lots of
little animals streaming out of the hand of God. But
one's turning back. He's had a look and decided to sit
this one out. It's really marvellous!

AUNT Your grandpa never understood such things, he
tried to pretend they were a silly waste of time. He

had no self-confidence, you see, that was the trouble; he was afraid to admit there were things he didn't understand. He used to say: "I have no strong feeling of confidence in myself. If I come into a room everybody will at once go out." And so he grew sadder and more impatient, and it was your mother who suffered most. Poor gentle creature, how she suffered.

STEVIE One day when I came home from school, I saw she was having a heart attack. I gave her some medicine, but there was nothing else I could do for her. She was very white in the face, and her lips were grey, and she couldn't breathe. And I was choked with fury and impotence, and choked with fears of helplessness and indignation. I raged against necessity, I raged against my very absent pa, I raged and fumed and spat. There was nothing else I could do.

AUNT *sighs.*

AUNT "Off to Valparaiso, love daddy." That's all we ever heard from your father. Picture postcards with foreign stamps.

STEVIE "Off to Valparaiso, love daddy." Yes.

AUNT When I grew too old for fairy tales, I started reading stories by minor Victorians with titles like "Mrs. Haliburton's Troubles" or "Lost Sir Massingberd." How richly compostly loamishly sad were those Victorian days, with a sadness not nerve irritating like we have today. How I love those damp Victorian troubles! The woods decay, the woods decay and fall, the vapours weep their burthens to the ground, man comes and tills the field and lies beneath, and after many a summer dies the swan.

MAN Wan
Swan
On the lake
Like a cake

Of soap.
Why is the swan
Wan
On the lake?
He has abandoned hope.

STEVIE Yes, always someone dies, someone weeps, in tune with the laurel dripping, and the tap dripping, and the spout dripping into the waterbutt, and the dim gas flickering greenly in the damp conservatory. "Behind the laurel bushes lay the corpse of Sir Vyvyan Markaby, baronet." Eventually, of course, Providence, tidies things up, yes, and keeps the right people on the right side of calamity. *(Rising)* Providence always did that in Victorian books; providence always tidied things up, and the heroines always preserved a stiff upper lip, smiling to the end, when God stepped in and made everything all right.

STEVIE replaces the book and sits in the desk chair. AUNT finishes slicing the beans, and rises.

AUNT Did you remember to get the sherry?

STEVIE Yes, it's in my bag.

AUNT observes some crumbs on the floor by the coffee table.

AUNT Just look at those crumbs. You wouldn't think I'd hoovered up in here this afternoon.

AUNT exits.

STEVIE The nurses said my mother died quickly in a minute. But how long is that minute?

Brief pause. STEVIE rises, picks up two sherry glasses from the piano, puts them on the coffee table, then takes a sherry bottle from her bag.

Did you hear about the death of the tigress Flo? She fell backwards into her pool at Whipsnade, and lay there in a fit. The pool was drained and Flo, that mighty and unhappy creature, was subjected to the indignity of artificial respiration. *(She pours sherry)* Yes, they worked Flo's legs backwards and forwards and sat on her chest. Sooner them than me, you'll say, and sooner me than Flo, that couldn't understand and wasn't raised for these high jinks. Back came Flo's fled spirit and set her on uncertain pads. She looked, she lurched, and sensing some last, unnameable, not wholly apprehended, final outrage, she fell, she whimpered, clawed in vain, and died.

Tender only to one
Tender and true
The petals swing
To my fingering.

Is it you, or you, or you?
Tender only to one
I do not know his name
And the friends who fall
To the petals' call
May think my love to blame.

Tender only to one
This petal holds a clue
The face it shows
But too well knows
Who I am tender to.

Tender only to one
Last petal's latest breath
Cries out aloud
From the icy shroud
His name, his name is Death.

STEVIE *turns, gazing at the silent* **MAN**.

The **MAN** *exits.*

STEVIE *puts the sherry bottle on the coffee table. She sighs, then switches on the lights.*

Sherry!

AUNT *(off)* What's that?

STEVIE I've poured the sherry.

AUNT *(off)* Just coming.

STEVIE *sits on the chaise, sips her sherry, and sighs pleasurably.*

STEVIE How lovely. Nothing nicer. Well not much. *(She chuckles)* There was once a woman called Miss Hogmanimy, which is certainly a name you'd want to get married out of. She had a bright smile, a highly polished face and an unprovocative blouse. She was terribly wrought up over B-A-B-I-E-S and the way they're born, and she gave up her whole life to going round giving free lectures, complete with lantern slides, to young girls of school or school-leaving age. She had a special way of talking, I remember, like losing her puff in an uphill climb, a sort of breathless whisper.

AUNT *enters.*

AUNT You're talking about that Miss What's-her-name.

STEVIE Hogmanimy.

AUNT Stupid woman. All that nonsense she used to talk.

STEVIE Her heart was in the right place.

AUNT Stuff and nonsense. Where's my sherry ?

STEVIE There.

AUNT *takes her sherry from the coffee table and sits in the armchair.*

AUNT Thanks. I don't hold with such things. You should've stayed at home.

STEVIE But of course I didn't. I went and sat in the school chapel with the other senior girls, eager to know exactly what happened.

AUNT Yes, I can see it all: giggling and laughing and carrying on.

STEVIE Fourteen-year-old, why must you giggle and dote,
Fourteen-year-old, why are you such a goat ?
I'm fourteen years old, that is the reason,
I giggle and dote in season.

AUNT People like Miss Thingummy do more harm than good, if you ask me. *(She sips her sherry)* What nice sherry!

STEVIE Tio Pepe.

AUNT Very nice.

STEVIE To listen to Miss Hogmanimy you'd think that knowing how B-A-B-I-E-S are born was enough to solve all the problems of adolescence. There'd be no more coming out in spots and getting self-conscious about the senior prefect, nor getting a crush on the English mistress, nor feeling proud and miserable like you do at that time, before you get grown up. She was always going on about the beauty of the human body, but I can think of a good many things a lot more beautiful. She kept saying: Oh how beautiful it all is, and how it's the holiest thing on earth, and she'd pray a prayer first of all, and we waited and waited and hoped we'd get the facts, but no it was all this funny breathless whisper. Being all tied up with love and religious sentiments, it was just impossible for her to get the medical side of the question across; she'd draw sections on the blackboard and stand her stout body in front of it, blushing furiously. The upshot of it was she wanted us to sign a paper saying that we'd never drink anything but ginger beer and cola and allied liquids.

AUNT You'd have been better off playing hockey.

STEVIE Poor woman, she tried hard but her wits were fuddled. I came away from the lecture with a profound aversion to the subject and a vaguely sick feeling when I heard of friends and relatives about to produce offspring. I used to pray for them and wash my hands of it, though at the same time I had plenty of deep down hopes that I wouldn't end up *intacta* like one of those depressed females that never get asked, never get the chance, and go around reeking with their unholy continence. As I grew older I guessed that copulation was probably first class fun, but I'd no idea how one actually set about it, nor indeed how one ever managed to find oneself a suitable mate.

AUNT Just like that girl in the paper.

STEVIE What girl?

AUNT Didn't I tell you? I'm sure I told you.

STEVIE Not a word.

AUNT Well this girl wrote to the paper and said she'd seen a young man at the tennis club she'd joined so as not to feel lonely, and to get herself fixed up with a young man and a house or a flat and a baby. Anyway, this young man would do, she thought, he was all right. The question was how could she get him to propose— they hadn't actually spoken, you see— so how could she make him propose? Well they published an answer and they said: "Arrange to play the last set with him and then linger hopefully and perhaps he will see you home."

STEVIE Oh, what a wonderful phrase! "Linger hopefully"!

AUNT "Linger hopefully and perhaps he will see you home."

STEVIE I can just imagine it, can't you? Up and down the suburbs, up and down the provincial towns, up and down India, up and down Singapore and Shanghai, there are girls who have arranged to play the last set and who are—lingering hopefully!

AUNT Lingering hopefully!

> **STEVIE** and **AUNT** laugh.

STEVIE Well thank God those days are over. No more hopeful lingering for me.

AUNT It wasn't all hopeful lingering, as I recall; there was quite a bit of sitting up in the bath, crying your eyes out over some boy or another.

STEVIE That was Freddy, he comes later. Karl was first.

AUNT Karl?

STEVIE You remember Karl. He arrived on Christmas Day with a potted flower for you, and a two-volume translation of "Faust" for me.

AUNT More books!

STEVIE And a dreadful translation it was.

AUNT Talking of Christmas reminds me of Miss Delabole. She was telling me that when the Dean of Westminster went into the Abbey for the early morning service one Christmas he saw only seven people were there. "Not enough," he said, and went home. *(She finishes her sherry and rises)* I'll just go and look at the meat. Best end of neck. Feeling hungry, Peggy dear?

STEVIE Yes, I am, rather.

AUNT *(picking up a pot of geraniums)* Good girl. Dear-oh-dear, those geraniums aren't very happy. I'll give them a drink of water.

> **AUNT** exits, carrying the pot of geraniums.

The clock chimes six. **STEVIE** *lights a cigarette.*

STEVIE At the foot of the Duke of York's steps Karl said: "I love you, Stevie." It was December. There was snow on the ground. "I love you, Stevie." Oh my sweet Karl, how I can see you now, with all of sleeping, happily dreaming Germany in your blue eyes. A student of philosophy at the University of Berling. *Ein student der philosophie.* Later we went into the country, we walked in the rain along a country road. There was a dead vole sticking its paws upright, like a Christian.

Now Vole art dead

And done is all thy bleeding.

We walked up a path towards a forlorn-looking empty house. Inside there was a musty smell reminiscent of murder, suicide and avarice. We found some sacking and lay down in each other's arms. "I love you, Stevie." He loved me, but he didn't like the English. I loved him, but I didn't like the Germans. "The Germans are neurotic," I said, "and weak. Look at Berlin swarming with uniforms and swastikas! They're cruel as well, with a vicious cruelty, not battle cruelty, but a doing-people-to-death-in-lavatories-cruelty. How evil is Germany today!"

Brief pause.

And so we quarrelled. And so we parted.

AUNT *enters.*

AUNT It won't be long now.

STEVIE Time for another sherry?

AUNT Yes, please.

STEVIE *refills the sherry glasses.*

You're smoking too much, Peggy. It's bad for you, bad for your tubes. Stevie The Lion Aunt always calls me Peggy, never Stevie.

AUNT What's wrong with the name you were christened with, I'd like to know.

STEVIE Nothing's *wrong* with it.

AUNT Well, then.

STEVIE Stevie started as a joke, really. Someone saw me out riding and thought I looked like Steve Donaghue, the jockey, you know. Steve became Stevie, and it stuck. *(She sits on the chaise)*

AUNT Peggy, you were christened and Peggy you shall remain. Where's the paper?

STEVIE It's on the desk.

AUNT *takes the newspaper, and sits in her favourite armchair.*

When I left school I went to Mrs Hoster's famous secretarial college, and then I got a job with Newnes, the publishers. I've been there almost the whole of my so-called ha-ha working life. All that capitalismus toil is very difficult and exasperating indeed, but my employers are kindly people and never complain about my writing during office hours. Actually, I've grown rather fond of my boss. He has a very dry sense of humour. I remember once telling him about a newspaper article which said that there were three million four hundred and thirty-two thousand five hundred and twenty-one illegitimate children in the United Kingdom. "Hoorah," he cried, "who says that England's going pansy?"

AUNT *speaks without looking up from her newspaper.*

AUNT Say what you like, I always thought you'd marry Freddy.

STEVIE *turns, puzzled by this non-sequitur.*

STEVIE What?

AUNT I can't think why you didn't.

STEVIE What on earth are you talking about?

AUNT *lowers her newspaper.*

AUNT And don't try to shut me up. I wasn't the only one, after all.

STEVIE Not the only what?

AUNT Person who thought you'd marry Freddy.

STEVIE *(rising)* Marriage, marriage, always this talk of marriage!

AUNT You made a fine old fuss when he went away.

STEVIE That's not the point.

AUNT What is, then?

STEVIE I'm not the marrying kind, I never have been.

AUNT You got engaged to him fast enough.

STEVIE I shifted my mother's ring onto my engagement finger, that's all. It was like a game, just a game.

AUNT Nonsense.

STEVIE I'm a friendship girl, not the marrying kind.

AUNT Stuff and nonsense!

STEVIE It's true! The very thought of marriage makes me nervous, it frightens me.

AUNT I've never heard such rubbish in all my life.

AUNT *loses interest in the argument, and disappears behind her newspaper.*

STEVIE She doesn't understand, she never has, and it's pointless trying to explain. I may look like a pocket Hercules, but I'm dreadfully low in energy, and a tired person like me just can't respond to love; either it's too much for her and she'd rather be dead, or else she sees it as a desperate chance clutch upon a hen-coop in mid-Atlantic. Oh, the fights and ecstasies of the spirit and the sad pursuing bones!

The **MAN** *walks briskly into the sitting room as the radio starts playing.*

MAN Am I too early?

Aunt puts down her newspaper and rises.

AUNT Freddy, dear, how nice to see you! *(She shakes hands with him)* I thought you were playing cricket.

MAN Rained off. Damn shame; I was rarin' to go. *(He mimes an off-drive)* Biff! Straight through the covers!

AUNT Come and sit down, dear. *(She sits)* What a pleasant surprise!

MAN *(sitting)* How are you, Miss Spear? Keeping well?

AUNT Oh yes, I mustn't grumble; well I do, but I shouldn't, you know how it is.

MAN I do indeed, I do indeed.

STEVIE rises and turns off the radio.

AUNT How are your parents ?

MAN Not too bad, all things considered. Dad's rheumatism's been playing up a bit.

Aunt and the **MAN** *continue their conversation in dumbshow.*

STEVIE They always made me feel very welcome in Freddy's house. Such kind, solid people. I was often invited to tea, after a walk, say. And there's his kind mother. And scones for tea. And they draw up to the fire and there's talk about how awfully common the other people in Palmers Green are being all the time. And how they have their dinners in the kitchen and sit in their shirt sleeves. Suburbs people are always ashamed of being suburbs people; they're always having to show that they're not like that themselves, oh no, not like the others, oh no, not like *that. (She sits on the coffee table)*

MAN They went up to town last week with the Westbrooks. You know the Westbrooks?

AUNT Yes, of course.

MAN They saw the new Jack Buchanan show, very good, they said. Dinner at the Troc afterwards, very jolly.

AUNT The Westbrook girl's getting married, isn't she?

MAN That's right, next month.

AUNT Such a pretty girl. I can't think why she wasn't married years ago.

She glares at **STEVIE**.

AUNT *and the* **MAN** *continue their conversation in dumbshow.*

STEVIE The people of Palmers Green have an idea, the unmarried girls have an idea, that if only they were married it'd be all right, and the married women think: Well now I'm married, so it *is* all right. Sometimes of course it is all right, but sometimes they have to work very hard saying all the time: So now I'm married, so now it's all right, so Miss So-and-so isn't married, so that's not all right. And the girls who are not married are often getting quite desperate, oh yes, they're becoming quite desperate, they're saying all the time: If only I was married, if only I was married. It's like the refrain in "The Three Sisters." It's the *leitmotiv* of all their lives. It is their Moscow.

MAN They're having a bit of a do next Saturday, a cricket club do, you know, drinks and so on.

AUNT Are you going?

MAN We're both going.

STEVIE Are we?

MAN Well yes, I took it for granted.

STEVIE You shouldn't take things for granted like that.

AUNT Why on earth not? You're engaged, after all.

> AUNT *and the* MAN *continue their conversation in dumbshow.*

STEVIE He'll have my heart, if not by gift his knife
Shall carve it out. He'll have my heart, my life.

AUNT *(rising)* I'll just go and prod the joint. Mint sauce or redcurrant jelly?

STEVIE I don't mind.

AUNT I thought you preferred redcurrant; I bought some specially.

STEVIE *(rising)* I really don't mind. You choose. *(She sits on the chaise)*

AUNT You are a difficult girl sometimes.

> AUNT *exits with the plate of cake and ginger nuts.*

MAN Pleased to see me?

STEVIE Well of course.

> *The* MAN *takes an apple from the fruit bowl.*

MAN Pity about this damn rain; I felt like a knock this afternoon. Mmm, nice apples. *(He munches the apple, grins at* **STEVIE,** *then sits by her on the chaise)* Give us a kiss and say you love me.

STEVIE Not now.

MAN She's in the kitchen, she can't see us.

STEVIE Your mouth's full of apple.

The **MAN** *swallows hard.*

MAN All gone.

The **MAN** *moves to embrace* **STEVIE**.

STEVIE *(rising)* No, Freddy, please.

MAN What's the matter?

STEVIE *(moving to the desk)* Nothing's the matter.

MAN You're in one of your moods.

STEVIE *(sitting at the desk)* I'm not in any sort of mood.

Pause.

MAN *(rising)* Is it because of, is it because of the other night? Is it?

No response.

You agreed, you said yes. I didn't make you do it. Did I?

STEVIE *shakes her head.*

What's wrong, then?

STEVIE Nothing.

MAN Don't be daft, something's wrong. What is it? Don't sulk, tell me.

STEVIE Why did you ask me if I was enjoying it?

MAN What?

STEVIE Right in the middle, you know, right in the middle of everything, you said: "Are you enjoying it?"

MAN Did I?

STEVIE "Are you enjoying it, dear?"

MAN Well sorry, I'm sorry. I didn't mean to offend.

STEVIE Don't *say* that!

MAN Don't say what?

STEVIE I'm not *offended*!

MAN What, then?

STEVIE It's so typical, can't you see? It's so suburban.

MAN Well I am suburban. So are you.

　　　The **MAN** *moves to embrace* **STEVIE**.

Come on, Stevie, it's nothing to get upset about.

STEVIE I'm not upset, I'm frightened.

MAN Frightened of old Freddy?

STEVIE Of getting married.

MAN Don't be such a chump.

STEVIE It's the truth. If I'm going to be a wife I want to be a good wife, and I don't feel up to being a good wife. It's my tubercular glands, I don't have the stamina. *(She rises, moves down, and kneels)*

MAN That's just an excuse. *(Pause. He squats beside her)* Don't you love me anymore?

STEVIE Part of me does.

MAN Well thanks very much.

STEVIE *(putting her arms round him)* Of course I love you, you're strong and safe and comforting. It's just...

MAN What?

STEVIE If we get married, I won't be Stevie anymore, I'll be Mrs Freddy. That's what frightens me.

MAN It's the same for any other girl.

STEVIE *(pushing him away)* I'm not "any other girl", I'm *me*. You take so much for granted!

MAN *(rising)* Like what?

STEVIE I don't know, everything. You expect me to behave in a certain way, to think in a certain way, to lead a certain sort of life. Well I don't think I can do it. I don't think I want to. *(She rises)*

The **MAN** *is silent; he stands gazing at* **STEVIE**.

I'm a friendship person, don't you see? The rhythm of friendship is strong in my blood: I must go, I must come back. Here I am again. Now I am going. I love people, but I love the thought and memory of them just as much. There comes a time when I have to go away, and then after a time, I must come back. It's a friendship rhythm, Freddy, I wasn't made for marriage. Don't you understand?

MAN Not a word. I don't know what the hell you're talking about.

STEVIE If only we could be friends.

MAN Friends? What do you mean, *friends*? Grow up, Stevie!

STEVIE Grow up?

MAN Yes, grow up! You're like a child, living with your aunt, cossetted night and day, that's not a proper way of life for anyone. And don't start all that nose-in-the-air-arty-bohemian nonsense; you know it doesn't wash with me.

STEVIE and the **MAN** *stare at each other.* **STEVIE** *turns away, bowing her head.*

STEVIE Oh, Freddy! How can we marry, how can we? It'd be utterly foolish, utterly suicidal!

MAN You can't mean that.

STEVIE Well I do.

The MAN *stands motionless, dumbstruck.*

MAN I see. Very well. If that's what you think.

STEVIE Don't you? Honestly, don't you?

MAN It could work. If you changed, it could work.

STEVIE Why me? Why should I change?

MAN You'll have to sooner or later, heavens above. Grown people don't spend their lives in a cocoon, writing poems with an old maid aunt.

STEVIE I don't like change.

MAN Then you'll be lonely.

STEVIE All right, I'll be lonely.

MAN You'll die alone, and you'll deserve to. Little pets like you deserve to be lonely.

STEVIE Oh go to hell.

MAN Go to hell yourself.

STEVIE Go to hell!

The MAN *exits, slamming the front door.*

Brief pause.

It's like escaping from a sunk submarine. You must stand quietly and without panic until the flood water in the escape room is covering your shoulders, is creeping up to your mouth, and only then when the whole of your escape room is flooded to drowning point will you be able to shoot up through the escape funnel, to shoot up for ever and away. Then it's over.

But when it's over, then it's tearing inside, it's "tearing in the belly", and one wishes oneself dead and unborn. *(She lights a cigarette)* When Freddy left, I ran a very hot bath and sat there, I just sat there in the water. And silently the tears fell down. I just sat there, my fringe all cock-awry, and the tears running down my cheeks into the hot water. *(She sits on the chaise)* It was as if the world had come to a sad, despairing, tearful end, but of course it hadn't. One does little things and goes to see friends and does one's work and fusses with this and that and feels in one's hearts the drift and dribble of penultimate things. Kind friends tell you that 'Time is the only doctor', and it's true. But he's a slow worker, that 'Time', and no anaesthetist at all. Suddenly you have lost everything, and the hours are long, and only a thousand hours will help to heal.

Would he might come
Again and I
Upon his breast
Again might lie.

Would I had not
In foolish wrath
Driven him ever
From my path.

Would the sun
His day's course over
Might that same day's
Lost dawn recover.

As vain as this
Vain prayers are all
Vain prayers that would
Past days recall.

Never shall sun
Now sunk away

Rise up again
On yesterday.

Never shall love
Untimely slain
Rise from the grave
And live again.

And so one is left bitter, resentful and lonely, with this
sadness deficiency feeling. I tend to think that many
people carry this feeling around with them for most
of their lives. A lot of people pretend, out of bravery I
suppose, that they're very dull and ordinary chaps, but
really they don't feel at all at home in the world, and
aren't able to make friends easily. Of course they joke
a lot and laugh, and their chums think they're quite all
right and jolly nice too, but sometimes they get tired
and the brave pretence breaks down and then they are
lost.

The **MAN** *enters to his chair down right.*

I wrote a poem about this once. I got the idea from a
newspaper report about a man drowning.

MAN Nobody heard him, the dead man,
But still he lay moaning:
I was much further out than you thought
And not waving but drowning.

Poor chap, he always loved larking
And now he's dead.
It must have been too cold for him his heart gave way,
They said.

Oh, no no no, it was too cold always
(Still the dead one lay moaning)
I was much too far out all my life
And not waving but drowning.

Silence. **STEVIE** *sits motionless.*

AUNT *(off)* Peggy dear, dinner!

   STEVIE *does not move.*

   (Off) Peggy!

STEVIE Yes, coming.

AUNT *(off)* Dinner's ready!

STEVIE Coming!

   STEVIE *exits.*

ACT II

The same. Evening.

The sitting room is empty and dark. The **MAN** *is sitting on his chair offstage down right, with a book of* **STEVIE** *Smith's poems.*

STEVIE enters. She is wearing her everyday outdoor coat over party clothes: a buttercup-yellow dress, silver lamé stockings and black patent-leather shoes with single straps. She switches on the lights at the radio table.

STEVIE Dear-oh-dear. Parties! I do love them, but really, so tiring. By the time I've got myself ready, I'm totally exhausted and arrive looking like the sheeted dead. "Miss Stevie Smith," they call out, and in I walk: the sheeted dead.

AUNT *(off)* Peggy!

STEVIE Yes, it's me!

STEVIE takes off her coat, and throws it on to the armchair back.

And I never know what to do with my hands. I keep thinking: But *what* shall I do with my hands? Plus, of course, the ghastly problem of finding the bathroom. Whenever I get excited, I always dash straight for the bathroom. Nervous enteritis, they call it. Straight to the bathroom! It's so embarrassing, especially with strangers.

AUNT *(off)* Peggy, is that you?

STEVIE It's me, I'm back! *(She pours herself a brandy)* The Lion Aunt's become a dreadful worrier, she worries about everything. She doesn't go out much either, well hardly at all. She thinks the house stood such a lot during the war that now it shouldn't be left. I know how she feels. It certainly stood an awful lot: the blitz, the doodlebugs, the V-twos. The Home Guard used to practise in the park, I remember, and there was a searchlight unit by the allotments. I became a fire-watcher, believe it or not, and used to patrol the streets near Trafalgar Square with my friend Norah Smallwood, who works for Chatto and Windus. *(She sits on the drinks table)* Someone said that the middle-classes were always the steadiest under fire. They didn't panic, you see, they were able to cope with the situation whatever it was. Well I'm glad about that. I'm a middle-class girl myself, conditioned by middle-class thought, and it's nice to know that we have our virtues. Heigh-ho, what a time it was, the war I mean, my word yes. There were some people called Rackstraw…

AUNT enters. She is wearing a plaid dressing gown.

AUNT I've been calling and calling.

STEVIE I thought you were just saying hello.

AUNT brandishes a buff-coloured envelope.

AUNT Look at this. Another letter from those Income Tax devils. You hid it in the fruit bowl.

STEVIE Well I don't suppose it's very important.

AUNT It looks important. "On Her Majesty's Service."

STEVIE What does it say?

AUNT I haven't opened it.

STEVIE Why not?

AUNT I was waiting for you. What are you drinking?

STEVIE Brandy. Do you want some?

AUNT No, I'll have a cup of tea.

STEVIE I'll get it, shall I?

AUNT You stay here, I'll get it. How was the party?

STEVIE Very jolly.

AUNT Good.

> **AUNT** *exits.*

STEVIE Yes, she's getting old, becoming an old lady. *(She sighs, and takes a sip of brandy)* I must be careful not to give the wrong impression. About being middle class, I mean. Suburbs people are extremely class conscious, and I don't approve of that, oh no. I was once in a terribly refined tea shop in Evesham when a poor dirty old man came in. He'd obviously made a mistake and didn't realize how refined this tea shop was. The tea shop lady was very snooty.

This Englishwoman is so refined
She has no bosom and no behind.

She took him gingerly by the coat sleeve, and led him to the door, she wouldn't have him there, no, no, it wouldn't do at all. The old man went shuffling out, drips falling down from his damp nose, and as he went out he said, "It's a fooking stook-oop tea shop." Sometimes I think it's a fooking stook-oop world, and quite often, I'm afraid, it's the middle classes who are the worst offenders. They're the ones who fight to the last ditch for the public schools and the privilege idea because they think they're so nearly about to clasp it, and so nearly about to send their kids to Eton. Never a thought for the kids, mind you, never a thought for the kiddos' welfare.
Parents who barely can afford it

Should not send their children to public schools ill will reward it.

AUNT *enters with an opened letter, a glass of milk and a plate of game pie.*

AUNT I found a bit of game pie in the larder. *(She puts the milk and game pie on the pouffe)*

STEVIE I thought you were going to have some tea.

AUNT What?

STEVIE You said you were going to make yourself a pot of tea.

AUNT Did I? I changed my mind.

AUNT *sits in the armchair, and takes out the Income Tax letter.*

STEVIE She keeps forgetting things.

AUNT What?

STEVIE Nothing.

AUNT Look at it, Peggy, just look at it. "Do you make any repayment claims?" Well do I?

STEVIE *(going and taking the letter)* Let me see. No, there's been some mistake. They think you're a man.

AUNT A man?

STEVIE They've called you Esquire.

AUNT Disgraceful.

STEVIE I shouldn't worry about it.

AUNT If cousin James was alive I'd get him on to this.

STEVIE Ignore it. *(She lights a cigarette and sits on the drinks table)*

AUNT He'd have known what to do.

STEVIE Cousin James. He was one of the high-ups in Somerset House, very clever, very conscientious, and rather severe. He was a socialist of the Huxley-antimacassar period, when it was considered the acme of a man's rights to work twelve hours a day, go to a night school free for another six, and then sleep for six hours on as hard a bed as could be found.

AUNT He'd have sorted this out.

STEVIE Yes, he probably would. He was always taking up the legal cudgels on her behalf.

AUNT Where's the writing paper?

STEVIE On the desk, but don't do it now. Do it in the morning.

AUNT Never put off till tomorrow what you can do today.

> **AUNT** *fetches her writing-paper, closes the door, switches on the main light, and sits at a table, writing a letter.* **STEVIE** *lights a cigarette.*

STEVIE What was I going to say? Oh yes, the Rackstraws' dog. It was during the war and these people the Rackstraws, they lived nearby, these people gave their dog to the Army to be trained for front line duties. But for some reason or another, may be it was one dog too many for them, this dog was sent back home. After the training was complete, he was sent back home. I remember now, it was an injury to his right forepaw, he was invalided out. The trouble was he'd been taught fierce ways, he'd been taught again his wolf behaviour, he'd been taught to fight and bite. So when his fond master went down the garden path to meet him, the dog leaped up, bared his fangs, and went to bite the throat of his loving friend. So the man clubbed him down with his heavy stick, so the dog died, and they buried him in the back garden. On his gravestone they wrote: "He died for King and Country."

AUNT How many Gs in aggravating?

STEVIE Two.

AUNT Two. Are you sure?

STEVIE A-G-G-R-A-V. Two Gs.

AUNT Well you ought to know, it's your job after all.

STEVIE *(rising)* The Lion Aunt has never approved of my writing. She doesn't disapprove either; she just thinks it's a waste of time, "soppy" as she calls it, a soppy waste of time. Well for years it was. I wasn't exactly a raging success in the thirties and forties, though I did manage to get my first novel published in nineteen thirty-six. I called it *Novel on Yellow Paper*.

AUNT You do think up some daft titles.

STEVIE I wrote it at the office, on the yellow paper we used for carbon copies.

AUNT That doesn't make it any less daft.

STEVIE Well some people liked it, lots of people actually, people *and* critics. For a time I was almost a Name to Conjure With.

AUNT Not for long, though.

STEVIE No, not for long.

> *The* **MAN** *rises and steps on to the stage.* **STEVIE** *sits on the desk chair.*

MAN Sudden fame and then oblivion. That must have been hard to bear.

STEVIE Hardly oblivion, my poems were still published. But you're right, it was hard; nobody likes being disregarded.

MAN It's important to you is it, public recognition?

STEVIE Of course; if you write something you want people to read it.

MAN And that's why a writer writes: to be acclaimed, to be recognized.

STEVIE Well it's a reason, I suppose, not the reason.

MAN What is the reason?

STEVIE Oh I don't know, I couldn't say.

MAN You must've thought about it, surely?

STEVIE Not really, no I haven't. If you think too much about your inspiration you find that you're quite unable to write at all. It's like digging up flowers to see how they're getting on. "Where the apple reddens never pry."

MAN I can't believe that a poem suddenly pops up and takes you by surprise.

STEVIE Oh but they do, yes they do.

MAN But there must be a reason why you start writing a particular poem. Is it personal experience, fantasy or what?

STEVIE I write for myself really, to get something out that's working away at me. The pressures of life, you know, and fancies: the pressure of daily life, the pressure of having to earn one's living, the pressure of one's relations with other people, the pressure of despair.

MAN What about happiness?

STEVIE Well it's not easy to get happiness into a poem, and often one doesn't want to. It spoils the fun. No, most of my poems get written from struggles and melancholy. Happiness is silent, or speaks equivocally to friends, Grief is explicit and her song never ends.

MAN One hears a lot about the dreadful agonies of creation. Do you find writing a painful process?

STEVIE Sometimes I do, sometimes I don't, it all depends. Of course there are those days when you think: I'm finished, I'll never write another word. Coleridge days, you know.

MAN With the Person from Porlock knocking on the door.

STEVIE Hammering's more like it. I do think he was a frightful cheat, don't you, Coleridge, blaming his bad days on some poor harmless visitor. I think he was already stuck in the middle of *Kubla Khan* and was just looking for an easy excuse.

I long for the Person from Porlock
To bring my thoughts to an end,
I am becoming impatient to see him,
I think of him as a friend.

It's difficult, you see—writing—it's a difficult business, difficult and exasperating. It can be very exasperating.

MAN And painful?

STEVIE Oh well sometimes it is, but I don't mind. "Out of the tears the poems come", you know how it is.

AUNT Yours faithfully. "Yours faithfully" indeed! What nonsense putting that, you never mean it. Where are the envelopes?

STEVIE Haven't they sent a label? They usually do.

AUNT Oh yes, so they have.

MAN You've published almost everything you've written. Do you ever regret this?

STEVIE Why should I regret it?

MAN Some of your work might seem to be a little unconsidered, a trifle hasty perhaps. Don't you wish you'd kept some of the poems until you could judge them more objectively?

STEVIE When people hoard their poetry it usually means they're afraid, afraid of criticism. It's a weakness not a strength. When a poem's finished it's finished as far as I'm concerned; it has its own existence and a right to see the light of day, which means that one must try to get it published. To do anything else is asking for trouble.

The monk sat in his den,
He took the mighty pen
And wrote "Of God and Men".

One day the thought struck him
It was not according to Catholic doctrine;
His blood ran dim.

He wrote till he was ninety years old
Then he shut the book with a clasp of gold
And buried it under the sheep fold.

He'd enjoyed it so much, he loved to plod
And he thought he'd a right to expect that God
Would rescue his book alive from the sod.

Of course it rotted in the snow and rain;
No one will ever know now what he wrote of God and men.
For this the monk is to blame.

AUNT *rises.* **STEVIE** *rises and moves to her.*

AUNT I'm off to bed.

STEVIE Sleep well, darling,

AUNT *(kissing* **STEVIE***)* And you, Peggy. God bless, happy dreams. *(She picks up the coat from the armchair and moves to the door)* "Yours faithfully", indeed! Stuff and nonsense!

AUNT *exits with the coat and letter.*

MAN I wonder how you place yourself as a poet. Do you think of yourself as being typical, a typical example of a contemporary poet?

STEVIE Typical? I don't know whether I'm typical, I don't know what that means. But then I'm alive today, therefore I'm as much a part of our time as everybody else; the times will just jolly well have to enlarge themselves to make room for me, won't they? And for everybody else. Being alive is being alive; being alive now is being alive now. *(She sits)*

MAN *(sitting)* Yes, but you deliberately shun contemporary verse.

STEVIE Do I? I wouldn't have thought so. Why do you say that?

MAN You never read modern poets; nothing since *Beowulf.* Didn't you say that?

STEVIE Only because I think it's dangerous. If you read too much, there's a danger you'll get your lines crossed and start writing other people's poems and not your own. It's not arrogance or anything like that; just self-preservation.

MAN And what about your own poems, what effect do you think they have on the people who read them?

STEVIE Oh I've no idea, none whatsoever.

MAN None at all ?

STEVIE None at all! I often look at a poem and think to myself: I don't know why anybody reads any of it.

AUNT *(off)* Peggy dear, I forgot the milk.

STEVIE Yes, it's here.

AUNT *(off)* Peggy!

STEVIE *(rising)* Yes, I'll bring it!

The **MAN** *rises.* **STEVIE** *picks up the glass of milk and the pie. The* **MAN** *starts to make notes on an envelope.*

I don't think these things matter very much, anyway; the whys and wherefores are beside the point. A poet should be made to get on with his writing and that's that, he should be put in a room with pencils and a pen or a typewriter, and be told to get on with it. And then if his poems are no good, he must be thrown out. A poet's not an important person; there'll always be another poet. *(She goes to the door)* Would you like a hot-water bottle? *(She turns out the main light)*

AUNT *(off)* Oh yes, please!

    STEVIE *exits.*

MAN And so, for most of her life, Stevie followed her own advice and just got on with it: a part-time poet. Every morning she caught the Piccadilly Line tube to her office near the Strand, and every evening she travelled back to Palmers Green, to Avondale Road, and to the Lion Aunt. Life is like a railway station, Stevie said. One day they brought her home early, in great distress. Her wrists were bandaged.

She took the knife
Its cruel edge would bite
Into her flesh
Had she the resolution or the art
To bear the smart
And drive it to her heart?

Death, that sweet and gentle friend, failed to respond to her summons. Life continued.

The **MAN** *steps off the stage and exits down right.*

The lights come up to day.

AUNT *enters with a blanket. She sits in the armchair and drops the blanket on the floor.*

AUNT Peggy! Peggy!

STEVIE *(off)* Just coming!

AUNT *tries to pick up the blanket.*

AUNT Tarnation take it! *(She reaches for the blanket, but it slips from her fingers)* Peggy, what *are* you doing? Peggy!

STEVIE *enters, wheeling a trolley of food. She is wearing a blouse, tweed skirt, ankle socks and sandals.*

STEVIE Here you are: a nice ham salad.

AUNT My soppy blanket's on the floor.

STEVIE So I see. Come on, let's tuck you up.

STEVIE *rearranges the blanket, then picks up the tray with ham salad from the trolley.*

There's a special treat for pudding.

AUNT What?

STEVIE Eat your salad first. *(She puts the tray on* **AUNT***'s lap)*

AUNT What is it, Peggy?

STEVIE A special treat. Eat your salad.

AUNT *begins to eat.*

She can't do much these days, poor darling, and it's up to me to run the house. She abdicated with great reluctance, as you can imagine. Now that I'm leading a domestic sort of life, I'd rather do the washing up than write. Housework's the most wonderful excuse for not doing anything else. I mean, clearing up a room, throwing everything away, it's marvellous. Then you're tired out, so you go to sleep all the afternoon. *(She goes to the trolley, and arranges the junket, cream and*

bowl, and the bacon rind on the top shelf) I love going out
and getting the food and chopping it up, hacking it
up. *(She fetches the empty brandy glass and puts it on the
trolley)* It's a wonderful way of getting rid of aggression!
When I write I write in the back room after tea. It's
a nice room, with a good view of the garden and the
birds. *(She turns to* **AUNT***)* Is everything all right?

AUNT Lovely, dear, thank you.

STEVIE Dearest Lion Aunt.
I will never leave you darling
To be eaten by the starling
For I love you more than ever
In the wet and stormy weather.

AUNT Tasty ham.

STEVIE It's York.

AUNT Yes, I thought so. Very tasty.

STEVIE Junket's her top favourite. Stevie's special junket.
When it's set, I grate nutmeg all over it and then add
a tablespoon of brandy or whisky. It's really delicious.

It was a house of female habitation,
Two ladies fair inhabited the house,
And they were brave. For although Fear knocked loud
Upon the door, and said he must come in,
They did not let him him.

And so we pass our days: housework, cooking, writing
and the occasional glass of sherry. I've retired now of
course, I retired early, and it's simply marvellous not
having to go into the office every day. I wasn't cut out
for the business world, I just didn't fit in. *(She opens
the window)* Lunchtime! Lovely bacon rind! Meal-o!
(STEVIE *throws the bacon rind into the garden and closes
the window)* No I never fitted in, like the little boy in
the commercial class who was told to try his hand at
commercial correspondence. "Dear Sir" he wrote,

"Sadly we see our customers falling away from us, but I hope that we shall always be friends. And so with love." They soon taught him business language, oh yes, he was soon corrected. But not me, not Stevie, I was always slightly out of step. I used to think I should've been a pirate or something, a North Sea pirate. We're all seafaring men in our family, after all, even my poor father. *(She sits in the desk chair)* It was good for me, though, the office routine, I needed the discipline. If I'd never had to work I'd have become some sort of invalidish person and never done any writing; it was exile from domesticity that produced my poems. I enjoyed a lot of it too, office life, oh yes. I loved the stock exchange language they used, with its curious religious undertones: conversion, redemption, pegged at sixty. Marvellous! It wasn't a taxing job either, far from it. I used to sit in my tiny office, writing poems and books, and asking my friends round for tea and hot-buttered toast. My boss never complained, never, never so much as gave me a reproachful glance, he was very kind. *(She chuckles)* He used to advise me about stocks and shares. "Have you anything in Gossards?" he'd say. "If you've anything in Gossards, then sell." My word, how we laughed. Dear Sir Frank, I can see him now: walking past my office door in dark dark mourning clothes and a dark dark top hat. He was forever going to funerals. "Another good man buried," he'd say, and walk on with sombre tread. *(Brief pause. She rises. The smile fades from her face)* There's not much to say about the suicide business; it's something I'd rather forget. It's too painful, too much remorse. *(She kneels at the drinks table)* Not because of the act itself, not just because of the act itself, no, one regrets the pain one inflicts on other people. Aunt. Sir Frank. My friends at the office. It shouldn't have happened there, not like that, poor Sir Frank was dreadfully upset. Upset, but not surprised, I doubt very much whether he was greatly surprised. "I'm rather disturbed about this death feeling in your poems, Stevie," he said to me once. He knew. Oh yes, he knew. *(She is silent for a moment; her head bows forward)*

AUNT I've finished. Peggy, I've finished.

STEVIE What?

AUNT It's all gone, every mouthful.

STEVIE Good, that's splendid. Now for pudding. *(She picks up the salad plate from* **AUNT***, goes to the trolley and brings the bowl of junket and the cream to* **AUNT***)* Here you are.

AUNT Junket! What a treat!

> **STEVIE** *pours cream over the junket.*

STEVIE And some cream to go with it.

AUNT How kind of you, Peggy. Oh you have been a busy girl. *(She begins to eat.)*

> **STEVIE** *sits on the coffee table and puts the cream jug on it. Her tone of voice is bright and animated, with no hint of suicidal despair.*

STEVIE Oh yes, I seem to be tremendously busy these days. I've got a lot of darling friends and I get entertained pretty freely, always dashing off to brasserie, bar, club and pub. Every so often, when Aunt's feeling well enough to cope by herself, I go week-ending in the country. I love it when people ask me back: "Do come again, Stevie." I think they're the best words of all. "Do come again."

> **STEVIE** *chuckles.*

AUNT This is delicious, Peggy.

STEVIE Good.

AUNT What a treat!

> **AUNT** *continues eating.* **STEVIE** *watches her with warm affection.*

STEVIE It was a little captive cat
           Upon a crowded train
           His mistress takes him from his box
           To ease his fretful pain.

           She holds him tight upon her knee
           The graceful animal
           And all the people look at him
           He is so beautiful.

           But oh he pricks and oh he prods
           And turns upon her knee
           Then lifteth up his innocent voice
           In plaintive melody.

           He lifteth up his innocent voice
           He lifteth up, he singeth
           And all the people warm themselves
           In the love his beauty bringeth.

           Some critics get awfully cross when I write cat poems,
           they seem to think it's letting the side down somehow.

AUNT Is there anymore, Peggy?

STEVIE I think you've had enough, don't you?

AUNT Just another spoonful, it can't do me any harm.

STEVIE All right, then, just one.

           STEVIE *serves a second helping of junket.*

           Don't eat it too fast and give yourself heartburn.

AUNT Thank you *very* much. What a lovely lunch!

           AUNT *resumes eating.*

STEVIE Lovely lunches follow lovely breakfasts and at night
            it's "God Bless, happy dreams." Nothing changes.
            Heigh ho! *(She puts the cream jug back on the trolley)* The
            other day I came across a copy of "King Solomon's

Mines" which I'd been given as a Sunday School prize, and on the paper cover at the back of the book I could still read my childish handwriting: Florence Margaret Smith, One Avondale Road, Palmers Green, North London, England, North-West Europe...

STEVIE
    The World. *(Speaking together)*
AUNT

STEVIE Well, I'm still here and so is Palmers Green, though it's now very large and bustling, and in a social sense I suppose its gone down. But really it's the same high lying suburb it ever was. The top of our hill is the highest spot between here and the Ural mountains, or so they say.

AUNT And so it is.

STEVIE So it is.

AUNT It is.

STEVIE And it's still a very active place: we've got our Art Circle, Shakespeare Reading Society, Players' Guild, the Library Discussion Group, tennis clubs, croquet clubs, swimming clubs, riding clubs, and branches of the Labour Party, the Liberal Party, the Communist Party and the Primrose League. We also have our fair share of intellectual revolutionaries. These people see the middle classes as obstructionist box dwellers whose only thought is for themselves and their families—as if that were not the common thought of the greater part of mankind. *(She takes the tray from* **AUNT** *and puts it on the trolley)* They're the salt of the earth, these free-blowing revolutionaries, but it's wise to remember that you can't make a diet of salt alone.

STEVIE wheels the trolley off, singing a familiar hymn tune to herself. She returns to see that **AUNT** *is beginning to doze.*

Of course life *has* changed, and there are many things I miss: the lantern lectures in the Parish Hall, the dark mysterious wonderful woods where Trespassers were Forbidden—and which is now a housing estate—and those brightly-painted advertisements that used to decorate the blank brick walls of our Swiss-chalet railway station: "The Pickwick, the Owl and the Waverley Pen, they come as a boon and a blessing to men." And there was a striking poster for Jeyes' Fluid, I remember: a nurse—with something, one feels, of Lady Macbeth in her character—was slowly washing her hands, with her eyes staring straight ahead. She knows that Jeyes' Fluid can never wash out that stain, but it might perhaps disinfect it.

A soft snore from AUNT *makes* STEVIE *look round.*
AUNT*'s head is lolling forward, and she is fast asleep.*

She used to be such a brisk, managing person, and now she sleeps her life away.

STEVIE *strokes* AUNT*'s cheek.*

There is little laughter where you are going, and no warmth. In that landscape of harsh winter, where the rivers are frozen fast and the only sound is the crash of winter tree-branches beneath the weight of the snow that is piled on them—for the birds that might have singing froze long ago, dropping like stone from the cold sky—there the soul is delivered to a slow death. *(Brief pause)* I don't mind much about survival, I mean, supposing we had to go on for ever, how awful! Without death, I don't think one could possibly endure life. It's an escape from pain, of course, but also an escape from pleasure too prolonged. It's rather like being drawn into a race of water before it gets to the waterfall, it gets quicker and quicker and more exciting; as you grow older the more exciting it becomes. I don't know why people are taught that Death is such a calamity, I think he must be rather a dish. Besides, we all have to go sometime.

AUNT *wakens, and looks around sleepily.*

AUNT Soon be time for a glass of sherry.

AUNT *removes her spectacles, and rubs her tired eyes.* **STEVIE** *takes the spectacles.* **AUNT** *sleeps. Pause.*

STEVIE I think of myself as an Anglican agnostic, if such a thing is possible. I was brought up in Anglican, and I still like it very much—I love the hymns!—I just don't believe it anymore. I reject the comfort and sweetness of Christianity because I feel that it's not true. And it's cruel, too, hideously cruel.

Is it not interesting to see
How the Christians continually
Try to separate themselves in vain
From the doctrine of eternal pain.

They cannot do it
They are committed to it,
Their Lord said it,
They must believe it.

So the vulnerable body is stretched without pity
On flames for ever. Is this not pretty?

The religion of Christianity
Is mixed of sweetness and cruelty
Reject this Sweetness, for she wears
A smoky dress out of hell fires.

Who makes a God? Who shows him thus?
It is the Christian religion does
Oh, oh, have none of it,
Blow it away, have done with it.

This god the Christians show

Out with him, out with him, let him go.

I suppose it's because we're so lonely, because Man is so lonely, that we must invent God. I think one should just accept loneliness, not make a theology out of it. If I'd been the Virgin Mary, I'd have said: "No, no, I'll have no part in it, no saviour, no world to come, nothing." *(Brief pause)* People think because I never married I know nothing about the emotions. They are wrong. I loved my Aunt.

STEVIE *leads* **AUNT** *off.*

The Lights fade, then come up to full.

The **MAN** *enters, assuming the persona of an urbane, slightly* **MAN** *nered literary-fringe figure. He carries a briefcase.*

MAN   I first met Stevie shortly after the war. Well, I say shortly, but in fact it was a little longer than that. A little longer than shortly. *(He takes notes out of his briefcase)* It must've been, at one of those noisy quasi-bohemian gatherings to celebrate somebody's book or somebody's exhibition or somebody's first night or somebody's something. All the familiar faces were there: Johnny Minton, Colquhoun and Macbryde, Tambimuttu, Maclaren-Ross. I was wondering how much longer I could put up with all that shrill chatter and cigarette smoke when I saw a strange-looking creature hiding in a corner and drinking gin with considerable verve. I went across and introduced myself. She gave me what can only be described as a radiant smile, and told me her name was Stevie Smith. I knew her work of course, and admired its quirky individuality. We had one of those brief shouted cocktail party conversations, mostly about the row Stevie was having with George Orwell, who had been her producer at the BBC. "He keeps lying to me," she said, "I'm bored to death by the lies."

STEVIE *(off)* Help yourself!

MAN What? *(He puts the notes back in his briefcase and leaves it in the armchair)*

STEVIE *(off)* Help yourself to a drink.

MAN Thank you, dear. *(He pours himself a gin and lime)* After a while, she asked me if I'd give her a lift to Palmers Green; it seemed rather a long way away, but I was grateful for the chance to escape. I soon learnt that she always expected her car owning friends to ferry her about, no matter how inconvenient it might be. God knows how many trips I've made on her behalf through the beggarly purlieus of north London! These rather tiresome duties have now reached a peak with Stevie becoming something of a star turn on the poetry reading circuit, which means a lot of travelling for Stevie and a certain amount of nervous exhaustion for her car-driving friends. Even so, my affection for her has survived, relatively unimpaired.

> **STEVIE** *enters, struggling to put on a tweed jacket.*

STEVIE Why, in a crisis, are one's coat sleeves always inside out?

MAN Let me help.

STEVIE No, no, I can manage.

> **STEVIE** *parades in front of the* **MAN**, *displaying a badly dyed green dress.*

How do I look?

MAN Very nice.

STEVIE That means you hate it.

MAN Not at all. It's very striking.

STEVIE I dyed it myself.

MAN So I see.

STEVIE "Caribbean Blue" it said on the packet, but it looks more greenish to me. What do you think?

MAN Well it's a bit patchy, Stevie, just a bit uneven.

STEVIE *(searching for something amongst the debris on the piano)* Oh that doesn't matter, they'll think it's part of the pattern or something.
With my looks I am bound to look simple or fast
I would rather look simple.
Anyway it's warm, that's the main thing. Those school halls are always so draughty.

MAN You should've worn trousers.

STEVIE Not me, darling, never trousers. Never trousers on principle.

   STEVIE *chuckles.*

   Did I tell you about that?

MAN Tell me about what?

STEVIE This Colonel I met at a hotel somewhere, Colonel Peck I think his name was, I could've hugged him. There was this lady, you see, this large English lady who always wore trousers. She wore them on principle, she told us at breakfast one morning. And a pretty fat principle too, said the Colonel. I could've hugged him! *(She finds what she is looking for, a brooch in tin box)* Ah, here it is. I knew I'd left it somewhere on the piano. *(STEVIE glances in a mirror)* Dear me, what a sight. I look a bit below par, don't I? A couple of sherries below par. Just like that ghastly photograph.

MAN What ghastly photograph?

STEVIE The one I showed you last week, the one that made me look as if I'd been dead for a very long time. I don't mind looking old, but I do have a thing about looking dead and buried. *(She turns to the* **MAN** *)* Brooch or necklace, which do you prefer?

MAN Either, Stevie, you look charming in either.

STEVIE Don't be so boring. Tell me what you think.

MAN I think we ought to hurry up. It's time we were going.

STEVIE Not yet, surely?

MAN It's gone half past.

STEVIE It won't take us more than a couple of hours.

MAN We ought to allow three.

STEVIE Two hours maximum, they said on the tephelone *(sic)*.

MAN The traffic gets bad at this time of day.

STEVIE Well we can't go yet, I haven't packed a bag. *(She goes to the desk, takes some notes out of a drawer)*

MAN What bag? You don't need a bag.

STEVIE I thought I'd take an overnight bag.

MAN What on earth for?

STEVIE Just to be on the safe side, you never know. *(She puts the notes in her handbag)*

MAN But we're driving straight back. That's why I'm here! We're driving straight back after the reading.

STEVIE You never know, darling, somebody might ask us to stay.

MAN Who? Who?

STEVIE People do sometimes, it's possible.

MAN I've got a meeting first thing in the morning.

STEVIE *(picking up her coat)* All right, come back, I'm not stopping you.

MAN Meaning you'll stay?

The MAN *helps* STEVIE *to put on her coat.*

STEVIE Well of course, if I'm asked. It'd be fun to have a party. It's so dull in London, don't you think, one never meets other writers, it's not like France, is it? Poets and writers don't go and sit in pavement cafés, it's not like Paris. Well the pavements are so awfully cold. And you can't just go up to people and say: "You're a poet and so am I, so I'm coming to dinner next Thursday."

MAN Stevie, this is ridiculous.

STEVIE What is?

MAN If you're staying overnight, you could've caught a train.

STEVIE I didn't say I *was* staying. I just said I'd like to.

MAN It's a bloody awful drive.

STEVIE You said it wasn't.

MAN A hundred miles there, a hundred miles back.

STEVIE Well you offered.

MAN You asked.

STEVIE You could've said no.

MAN Look, I'm driving up because there's no train back tonight...

STEVIE Yes and I'm very grateful, I told you I was grateful, I don't know what more I can say.

MAN Then why all this talk of staying overnight?

STEVIE I only mentioned it as a possibility.

MAN You should've told me before.

STEVIE I won't ask you again, don't worry. Never again, never, never, nevermore. Quoth the Raven. *(She pours herself a gin)*

MAN What are you doing now?

STEVIE Having a drink, what does it look like? *(She sits on the chaise and sips her gin)* It's not very kind of you, carrying on like this. How was I to know you'd want to get back straight away? I didn't know you went to meetings and things. It's very upsetting. *(She sips her gin)*

MAN All right, I'm sorry. *(He goes to **STEVIE**)* I'm sorry. Let's stop this bickering, shall we?

STEVIE I'm not bickering.

MAN Let's get a move on, then, otherwise we won't get there at all.

STEVIE Well I'm ready. I was ready ten minutes ago.

MAN I thought you wanted to pack a bag?

STEVIE There's no point, is there, if we're driving straight back. *(She goes to the door)* I'll just get the food.

MAN What food?

STEVIE I bought some sausage rolls; I thought we'd need a snack on the way. We'll take some glasses, too. Have a drop of gin.

> **STEVIE** *exits, carrying her glass of gin.*

MAN Dear, darling Stevie. She needed to be cherished, she needed to be lapped in loving care.

In the midst of *so* much love
And such comfort
Still to feel unsafe and be afraid,
How one's heart goes out to you!

I remember once sitting at the back of a cheerless school hall while Stevie pranced about on the stage, chanting her poems like an elderly Shirley Temple. It should've been embarrassing, but it wasn't; it was touching, truthful and haunting, and the school children were enthralled. She spoke to them directly, you see: from child to child, from heart to heart.

STEVIE *(off)* I thought you were in a hurry!

MAN Coming, Stevie.

STEVIE *(off)* Don't forget the gin.

The **MAN** *picks up the gin, and exits.*

The lights come up to day. The sitting room is empty. The clock chimes.

STEVIE *enters with a new coat, a new hat, a new silk scarf, two handbags, and a new pair of gloves. She is limping slightly. She puts the new clothes on the armchair.*

I've got a bad leg. What a bore. *(She sits in the desk chair and begins transferring the contents of her old handbag into the new one)* It was quite awful, I had to do a broadcast for the BBC and I told them about the leg, quite casually, you know. Well they sent a car for me *and* a rug. All I needed was a shawl and a hot water bottle to complete the picture! Everything has its compensations, I suppose, even getting old. Of course, I miss Aunt dreadfully. When you live with an old lady from an early age you never cease to be a child. Now she's gone and I find I'm old myself. Some people thought I should move: "Why don't you get a flat in London?" they said, but I didn't want to, I didn't want to leave Avondale Road. Everybody's so kind to me here, I'm better off in Palmers Green, and I've got used to living alone, oh yes, I quite like it. It's wonderfully dreamy to be in a house all by yourself; you can wander around and sleep in a different room every night if you want to. And if I'm tired, I just stay in bed. It's extraordinary how unaware one is of time passing. Some days are long and thin and there is nothing in them, but they speed past just the same. And suddenly you realize how short it all is, life, and how at the end comes death with the pleasure of certainty. *(She rises)* I read a lot these days, I read more than ever, Gibbon especially. *Decline and Fall* is my favourite book, I never tire of it. *(She goes to the mirror— puts a scarf and hat on)* I like Agatha Christie, too. I love reading her stories in French, it makes it all so wonderfully funny: *"Je suis un detective. Je m'appelle HerculePoirot."* I think she's a genius. *"Preparez vous à reçevoir un choc: votre patron, Mr Rachett, est mort!"* Her murders are so polite! *(She starts putting on her new coat)* Oddly enough, life has suddenly become rather exciting, and I'm now quite a celebrity. I've been photographed for the papers, I've been interviewed for the television, I've made gramophone records, I've lectured, I've even had my portrait painted. Mind you, it wasn't much like me, I didn't think so anyway. The colouring was lovely, but the lower part of the face seemed to belong to somebody else. To Disraeli, I think.

She sings.

DO TAKE MURIEL OUT
SHE IS LOOKING SO GLUM DO TAKE MURIEL OUT
ALL HER FRIENDS HAVE GONE.

ALL HER FRIENDS ARE GONE
AND SHE IS ALONE
AND SHE LOOKS FOR THEM WHERE THEY HAVE
    NEVER BEEN
AND HER PEACE IS FLOWN.

DO TAKE MURIEL OUT
ALTHOUGH YOUR NAME IS DEATH
SHE WILL NOT COMPLAIN
WHEN YOU DANCE HER OVER THE BLASTED HEATH.

She picks up the new handbag.

The most exciting thing of all was getting the Queen's Gold Medal for Poetry. This was a tremendous honour and I was tremendously pleased about it and very flattered too. It used to be sent by post, I believe, but Cecil changed all that when he became Poet Laureate, and quite right too. Just imagine getting a gold medal from the Queen with all those gas bills and postcards from Felixstowe! "Anything in the post today, dear?" "Oh just a gold medal from the Queen." Anyway, they told me to get to Buckingham Palace at such-and-such a time, and of course I was terrified of being late. I'm always late for everything. I had a fortifying drink at the Ritz and then walked through the rain to the Palace. I got there desperately early and they were still in the middle of Changing the Guard, so what to do? The only thing I could think of was to go next door to the Queen's Gallery, where I bought a whole lot of postcards, da Vinci drawings, which I had to cram into my handbag, it's not very big as you can see. So there I was, with a handbag full of postcards, standing in the rain outside Buckingham Palace. I walked up to one of the policemen and said, "I'm supposed to be in there, you know, I've got an appointment with Her Majesty to have this medal." To my surprise, he knew all about it and in I went, into the Palace. I was met by a rather decorative young man in naval uniform, and he took me into an outer room, whatever it's called, a huge room, and there was this lady-in-waiting, a most agreeable girl, and we had a very giggly time. She asked me to do a poem, so I hissed a short one under my breath, the one about a poor débutante sitting alone at a grand ball. It seemed appropriate, I thought.

I cannot imagine anything nicer
Than to be struck by lightning and killed suddenly crossing a field
As if somebody cared.
Nobody cares whether I am alive or dead.

My word, yes, we had a very jolly time. I adored that part of it. Then the one before me came out: a staggering looking woman. Heavens, I thought, I'm not properly dressed for this—I found this hat in a jumble sale, only five shillings, a tremendous bargain, but perhaps a bit of a mistake. Anyway, the young naval man took me to the door, and there far far away—the room's as big as Trafalgar Square—standing against the mantelpiece, was this charming figure, the Queen. I'd never seen Royalty close to before, well only once before. I saw the Queen Mother at the Book Prints Exhibition. I was standing on the first floor landing, and she walked below me. I could've poured sherry on to her hat. So there she was, there was the Queen. You curtsy and make your way across the room; then she comes forward and smiles, she's got a very gracious smile, and gives you the medal. As she gave it to me she said, "I don't know what you'll do with it." I looked at it and said, "Well I suppose I could have a hook put on it and wear it round my neck." "I don't know whether it's real," she said. "Oh," I said, "I'm sure it is." Then she motioned me, I think that's the expression, she motioned me to sit down. There was a table between us. They'd told me outside not to worry about when to come out because she'd ring a bell under the table. Well the poor darling kept on asking me questions about poetry, and I got the impression it wasn't exactly her favourite subject. "How do you think of a poem?" she asked. "Well," I said, "it just sort of comes to you, often when you least expect it. Right in the middle of hoovering, you know, you suddenly think of a poem." She made me feel awfully like a schoolgirl again, being interviewed by a rather cordial headmistress. After a while I got a bit nervous and said, "I don't know why, but I seem to have written a lot about murder lately." This was obviously the wrong thing to say; the royal smile got rather fixed. When it's all over you walk out backwards, curtsey at the door, and the young naval man gets a taxi for you. We went to the Epicure afterwards for a celebration lunch: Cecil Day Lewis, Eric Walter White— from the Arts Council— and

Norah Smallwood, my fire watching chum from
Chatto's. Dear Eric ordered oysters, which was a great
mistake; they took ages to arrive, and I had to ask the
waiter for some bread and jam to stave off the pangs.
Then back home to Avondale Road, *(She is silent for a
moment, smiling at the memory)* I so wished that the Lion
Aunt could've been alive to see it. Perhaps she'd have
changed her mind about my writing. Perhaps not.
Stuff and nonsense! Perhaps she was right, heigh-ho.
*(**STEVIE** chuckles. She stands motionless, a frail figure in her
best clothes, with the jumble sale hat pulled down over her
fringe of hair)*

*The **MAN** enters from down right.*

STEVIE *sits in the armchair.*

I have a friend
At the end
Of the world.
His name is a breath

Of fresh air
He is dressed in
Grey chiffon. At least
I think it is chiffon.
It has a
Peculiar look, like smoke.

It wraps him round
It blows out of place
It conceals him
I have not seen his face.

But I have seen his eyes, they are
As pretty and bright
As raindrops on black twigs
In March, and heard him say:

I am a breath

Of fresh air for you, a change
By and by.

Black March I call him
Because of his eyes
Being like March raindrops
On black twigs.

But this new friend
Whatever new names I give him
Is an old friend. He says:

Whatever names you give me
I am
A breath of fresh air,
A change for you.

Pause.

MAN Stevie's sister Molly suffered a severe stroke, which left her virtually helpless. Anxious to do what she could, Stevie packed her bags, said goodbye to Avondale Road and went to Devon, to Buckfastleigh, where Molly lived. It was there that she became ill. From Torbay Hospital she wrote to an old friend.

STEVIE Dear John, I am ill now, which means I have to stay down here until the doctors finish with me. I keep having sort of fits mixed with some poisoning down below ha ha. When the fits come I am almost un-consaince *[sic]* with something coming upon me, cannot speak proper words or read them, it is a nightmare of muddle of words and frightful bells ringing and unknown crowds crying out advice, warnings, etcetera that I cannot understand, or when sanity returns remember. I am now with two doctors and have to go at once to a third who is a specialist as soon as possible. When the doctors have spent ages and ages and mornings and mornings and afternoons and afternoons, dear, stick with sticks and glass tubes and being rather sharp with steel rods, then they'll know what's the matter! I'm not sure I'll be very bright ha ha as so often I cannot speech *[sic]* properly I scramble velly velly well. Do forgive me dear John if I've been already over and over all this again and again. I hope you are beautifully happy. Love, Stevie.

MAN The doctors diagnosed Glioblastoma, a tumour on the brain. She lost the power of speech.

Pause.

Stevie was sixty-nine when she wrote her final poem. Unable to speak, she scrawled a circle around one word.

I feel ill. What can the matter be?
I'd ask God to have pity on me,
But I turn to the one I know, and say:
Come, Death, and carry me away.

Ah me, sweet Death, you are the only god
Who comes as a servant when he is called, you know,
Listen then to this sound I make, it is sharp,
Come Death. Do not be slow.

The **MAN** *remains motionless.*

The lights fade, as— the curtain falls.

FURNITURE AND PROPERTY LIST

Set design from the original production of Stevie

ACT I

On stage: Black upright chair set down right off rostrum

3 dining chairs round dining table

1 dining chair below desk

Wooden chair with arms. *On it:* cushion

Armchair. *On it:* antimacassar

Chaise. *On it:* 3 cushions

Desk. *On it:* table lamp, letter rack with notepaper, blotter with 2 letters and paper knife, pen in Coronation mug, ashtray. *In drawer:* poetry notes. *As dressing:* stationery, notes, magazines, paperweight, ornaments, framed photograph

Desk chair

Table. *On it:* telephone, 1950 directory

Dining table. *On it:* chenille table cloth, lace table cloth, pot plant, fruit bowl, with apples and Aunt's spectacles, ashtray, watering can

Occasional table. *On it:* radio, geranium in pot, 3 books

Drinks table. *On it:* magazines, books. *On shelf under it:* 3 glasses, bottle of sherry, magazines

Coffee table. *On it:* lace cloth, ashtray

Bookcase. *On top:* wooden box, books, shells, ornament. *On shelves:* books, including one on Tintoretto

Piano. *On it:* 5 sherry glasses, Victorian tin with cameo brooch in it, clock, vase with bullrushes and honesty, littered piles of books, framed photographs, ornaments

Piano stool

Pouffe

On window ledge: 6 pot plants

On floor: piles of books round desk, piano, chaise and drinks table, wastepaper-basket full of rubbish by desk

On walls: mirror, framed watercolours

Lace window curtains, pink drape curtains (to be opened from offstage), set open

Offstage: Plastic shopping bag with full bottle of Tio Pepe sherry (**STEVIE**)

Tiered plate with Battenburg cake and ginger nuts (**AUNT**)

Tea tray with cloth, teapot, milk jug, 2 cups, 2 saucers, spoons (**AUNT**)

Newspaper (**delivered through letterbox**)

Bowl with beans, colander and knife (**AUNT**)

Apron with nail buffer in pocket (**AUNT**)

Personal: **STEVIE** handbag with cigarettes, matches, keys

MAN pencil, spectacles, watch

ACT II

Strike:

Watering can, shopping bag, handbag, cigarettes, matches, letters, newspaper, sherry glasses, Tintoretto book, sherry bottle

Set: Window curtains closed

Gin, lime juice, brandy, Tio Pepe bottles under drinks table

2 extra glasses under drinks table

STEVIE Smith poetry book with envelope on black chair

Calendar on wall above piano

4 piles of books on piano lid

STEVIE Smith drawings on piano lid

1960 telephone directory to replace 1950 one

Extra plants and books on floor

Offstage: Sealed Income Tax envelope (**AUNT**)

Open Income Tax envelope with label and letter (**AUNT**)

Blanket (**AUNT**)

Plate with game pie and glass of milk (**AUNT**)

Briefcase with notes in it (**MAN**)

Trolley. *Top shelf:* tray with cloth, napkin in ring, knife, fork, dessert spoon, plate of ham salad. *Bottom shelf:* bowl of junket with serving spoon, cream jug, dessert bowl, plate with bacon rind and knife (**STEVIE**)

LIGHTING PLOT

Property fittings required: pendant lamp, desk lamp, table lamp interior. A sitting room. The same scene throughout

ACT I

To open:	Blackout	
Cue 1	As CURTAIN rises	(Page 1)
	Fade up tableau lighting	
Cue 2	As Cue 1 completed	(Page 1)
	Fade up on Man	
Cue 3	Man: "…in the country."	(Page 1)
	Snap up full lighting, late afternoon	
Cue 4	Aunt: "Fate, indeed!"	(Page 6)
	Fade up on Man	
Cue 5	Man: "…tuberculosis."	(Page 7)
	Fade down on Man	
Cue 6	Stevie: "…that's how…"	(Page 8)
	Fade up on Man	
Cue 7	Man: "…such seas."	(Page 8)
	Fade down on Man	
Cue 8	Stevie: "…have a horror…"	(Page 12)
	Fade up on Man	
Cue 9	Man: "…loving husband, Wilfred."	(Page 12)
	Fade down on Man	
Cue 10	Stevies "…the soul stream."	(Page 13)
	Fade up on Man	
Cue 11	Man: "…one of many."	(Page 15)
	Fade down on Man	
Cue 12	Aunt: "…lies beneath…"	(Page 17)

ACT II

Lightning Source UK Ltd.
Milton Keynes UK
UKOW06f0337050315

247233UK00001B/2/P

Cue 30	As Stevie closes door behind them	(Page 56)
	General fade up	
Cue 31	As Man picks up gin bottle	(Page 56)
	General fade down—pause—fade up to previous lighting	
Cue 32	As Stevie moves to sit in armchair	(Page 66)
	Fade down to light focussing on armchair	
Cue 33	Man: "Do not be slow."	(Page 68)
	Fade to Blackout	

EFFECTS PLOT

ACT I

Cue 1	Aunt: "…just what she did."	(Page 5)
	Click of front door letterbox as paper delivered	
Cue 2	Aunt: "I'll give them a drink of water."	(Page 23)
	Clock chimes six	
Cue 3	Stevie: "…ecstasies of the spirit…"	(Page 27)
	Fade in radio music	
Cue 4	Stevie turns radio off	(Page 27)
	Snap off radio music	

ACT II

Cue 5	Man: "Life continued."	(Page 47)
	Open window curtains from offstage	
Cue 6	As lights come up to day	(Page 47)
	Clock chimes three-quarters	
Cue 7	Stevie: "…heigh-ho,"	(Page 52)
	Fade in music	
Cue 8	Stevie: "Being like March raindrops"	(Page 67)
	Fade out music	